Horse Not Zebra

Also by Eric Nelson

Some Wonder
The Twins (chapbook)
Terrestrials
The Interpretation of Waking Life
The Light Bringers
On Call (chapbook)

Horse Not Zebra

Eric Nelson

Terrapin Books

Terrapin Books
4 Midvale Avenue
West Caldwell, NJ 07006

www.terrapinbooks.com

ISBN: 978-1-947896-54-3
Library of Congress Control Number: 2022930867

First Edition

Cover art by Laura Berendsen Hughes
Shake the Yellow Leaves from the Bough of Your Heart—Rumi
acrylic painting on canvas, 30" x 40"

www.laurahughespaintings.com

for my family
especially the newest member
Lowell Sinclair Cartright-Nelson

Contents

I.

Clearing the Air   7
Almost Enough   8
Baton   10
My Alarm   12
Sheltered in Place   13
Earth as It Is   14
Not Here Not Here   16
Soap Spell   18
Switchback   20

II.

Gold   25
When Water Is Up to Here with Us   26
Mulch   28
Shrine   30
Lullaby to a Black Bear   32
By Campfire   34
Zen Dog   36

III.

Horse Not Zebra   39
Disclosure Statement   40
The Bus of History (Montgomery, Alabama, 1963)   42
Expecting Lowell   44
Washing Dishes at the Arsenal   46
Perfect Work   48
Aubade with Bear   50

IV.

All Evidence   53
Based on Actual Events   54
Biography of My Name   56
Blue Birds   57
Graying   58
Play Ball or Sing   60
About Black Bears   62

V.

Mysteries of the Ellipsis   67
Dark Evergreen   68
Parade   69
Never Good   70
Scouts   72
Rules of the Body, A Partial List   74
Disappearing   75
Avoiding the Dog   76
My Brothers   77

VI.

Beating Myself Up   81
Their Romance   82
Twelfth Night   84
The Day She Left   85
Live Like a Bear Is Near   86
The Runners   88
Bus Real   90
Blind Mover   92
The Creature   94

Acknowledgments   95
About the Author   99

I.

Clearing the Air

He's drifting out of the woods, head bowed,
right arm raised and waving slowly,
the way someone in church reaches God.
About my age, he's dressed as I am—cargo shorts,
t-shirt, low rise hikers—a version of me approaching me,
and I'm touched to witness his communion,
the summer foliage an eternity of tunnels and arches,
the sun-mottled trails scrolling through trees
like illuminated script.

As we near each other, he smiles a little sheepishly.
Lowers his arm and says, *Don't worry, I've cleared
the air for you*. Now I see he wasn't praying
but shielding his face from webs. On his sleeve
an orb weaver scrambles toward his neck. I don't
tell him. I feel wronged somehow. Not that I care
about the webs or spiders. They'll be back
tomorrow, but floating from the woods that way,
head down, arm up—I wanted a seeker returning

from wandering, answer in hand. Then a branch
snapped me back to me in the woods with the dog
as I am every morning, thinking to-do's, minding
the poison ivy, urging the dog to his business.
No epiphany in sight, no holy whispers in the canopy.
Yet I keep yearning for them, and already
I'm envisioning tonight—spiders stringing the trees
not with sticky traps, but with an array
of harp-like instruments tuned by wind and dew.

Almost Enough

Like that rainy night after poker when Jim backed his car
off the driveway into the ditch, and the five of us
pushed first from the back, then from the front, then

side to side, each time thinking the wheels were about
to spin free. When we gave up, the car was stuck
deeper in the muck and our shoes were caked.

Or the time the fallen maple blocked the greenway
and two joggers, a dog walker, and a biker leaned in
to shoulder it enough to make a small passage

but only managed to break off a limb and nearly crush
the dog. Or when the stone bench caved in
after the hurricane washed out the ground beneath it;

there were enough of us to right the legs, but when
we lifted the granite slab to reseat it, someone's grip slipped
and it sank into the soaked ground like a grave marker.

There were almost—but not quite—enough of us writing
letters and calling for swing sets instead of asphalt, parks
before parking lots, the woods rather than condos called The Woods.

Almost enough voted against coal ash pits and pig waste ponds
so hurricanes of the new climate won't sweep ash and shit
river by river to the ocean, fish rising up dead as they go.

There's almost enough of us to wipe oil from a thousand gulls
before they suffocate, almost enough to drag dolphins back
into water deep enough for them to dive away from us, almost

enough of us to pull the arrows from the eagle's grasp,
pass the dimmed lamp to the smallest hands, almost enough
to save, a bucket at a time, the house from burning down.

Baton

Even the bluebird fades
to gray as summer burns out.

The hawk's fearless screech
sounds more like grief exhausting itself.

I spend the afternoon deadheading
daylilies until my fingers numb, my back

and knees petrify. I remind myself that
new blossoms will blaze the path tomorrow,

and the stressed sugar maples I planted
in spring are tipped with new growth.

I lift a handful of mulch to my nose, breathe
the trees inside. And here comes the old couple,

climbing the steep street. He's frail and stooped
but setting a steady pace, one arm reaching

back, hand open as if waiting for a baton
to be placed in his palm by the woman

following him. She's taller and stronger
looking, her beacon-red hair piled so high

I think at first it's a hat. Arm outstretched,
she slips her hand smoothly into his and seems

to glide to his side. As they pass me they wave
as if they are the liberators of Barnard Avenue.

On the man's red sweatshirt is a silkscreened face
that looks familiar, but I can't place it until I see

the single word above the flowing black hair
and dashing beret: Che. No last name needed.

I think the sweatshirt must be as old as the man
himself, throwback on top of throwback, embers

of revolutionary fire. But then I realize it's new,
unfaded, still a little stiff. And the look on his face

isn't wistfulness or irony, it's devotion
to a future he won't see any more than I will

see the struggling maples grow tall enough to shade
the house in summer. How can I not raise my mulch

encrusted fist in salute, my flagging will surging
like a relay runner reaching out to hand off the baton?

My Alarm

isn't my neighbor's boots, though he stands on his porch
every dawn and slams them together repeatedly, dry muck
flying like dark sparks. Sometimes it sounds like the woodpecker
that beats its head against my house. Sometimes a drumstick
rapping a snare's rim, sometimes a gavel demanding order.

He pulls on the boots, double knots the laces, and drives off
to his landscaping job. Sure, there's days I pillow my ears.
But the sound of his two boots clapping is reassuring—
a sturdy, reliable answer to the news raging from the radio,
relentless as gunfire and wildfire. No, my alarm began long before

my neighbor. Today, it's twenty-three species declared extinct.
Yesterday, record overdoses and evidence that summers burn
hotter and longer than ever, spring and fall collapsing into one
long winter. Every day, I walk past a fake gravestone some
guerilla installed on the greenway, *R.I.P.* hand-lettered across

the top, and underneath: *We don't deserve paradise anymore*.
I think of my neighbor at his work planting trees, making paths.
Amending and mulching. At the end of the day, the last bed made,
he's back on his porch, sweat-stained and beat, pushing the muddy
boots off, leaving them at the door, heels up, to harden by morning.

Sheltered in Place

Possum scamper on the front porch.
Two great horned owls nest at the edge
instead of deep within the woods.
A black bear stands looking in the kitchen window
like it's casing the place for a smash and grab.

They're checking on us. Wondering, in their way,
why we've gone quiet. Why we appear as they do,
cautiously, before light, faces hidden. Hoping,
however they hope, we've changed. For their good.
The moon has come closer, too. It's larger. Brighter.
The man in it gone.

Earth as It Is

At the eclipse party, veil-like clouds
drift in at the same time someone
hands out champagne in plastic cups
and toasts the mysteries of the universe.
I raise my cup while putting on my shades

and spill champagne over my shoulder,
miraculously not getting any on me.
Everyone else is looking to the heavens
so it's like it didn't happen. Through the veil
of clouds and shades, the sky looks unreal

and symbolic. The black sphere sliding over
the orange sphere could be the wild, unconscious
mind blocking the self-centered, rational mind.
Or a glimpse of perfect union behind the illusion
of separation. Or else it's the moon and sun

we've known all our lives crossing paths,
and we don't have to pray or go blind to love
everyone staring up, mouths agape, empty
cups scattered like stars on the silvery grass.
Later, the sun ablaze again, the moon nowhere,

while I water the drooping garden I have a vision
of the note pinned above the kitchen sink
last year at the meditation retreat—
before enlightenment, washing the dishes.
after enlightenment, washing the dishes.

Not Here Not Here

1.
Still night when my morning walk takes me
to an unfamiliar block, I look
through a diner's dark window to a gleaming
slice of kitchen, clouds roiling from three
pots on the stovetop. There must be a cook
pulling ingredients from the walk-in,
but all I can see past the silhouettes
of chairs on tables is the pots and steam.

Now light speeds across the ceiling and bends
over me through the plate glass. The OPEN
sign snaps on before my eyes. A big man
in well creased whites appears and waves me in
like he knows who I am. A familiar
panic grips me; I back off into dawn.

2.
Just dawn when I enter the woods, I don't
see it, nearly step on it, the snake I think
is alive, then dead—until it hisses, whips
into a coil, lifts its head and fixes me.
Petrified, at last I let go a breath
and hurry on, quick as adrenaline.
When the trail circles back, I watch for it.
Not here. Not here. Then I flinch at a screech

above me. Pedestalled on a low limb,
talons gripping the snake, the hawk leans
forward, blinks, and shrieks again, warning me
I'm nothing to do with them--hawk, snake, woods—
and sweeps into the air, the morning sky
the same pale shade as the snake's underside.

Soap Spell

Gather your soap
Bring out your soap—
Scented and unscented
Dish and laundry
Homemade and factory made
True soap and beauty soap
Lye soap and soft soap

Cold press and triple milled
Soap of plants and oils
Soap for waking and soap for sleeping
Soap on a rope
Soap that floats like hope

Soap made of bark and roots
Of shells and high tide
Soap of the moon and the Milky Way
Soap that burns and soap
Of no more tears

Soap bubbled and blown
Into rainbowed ovals
Bursting for no reason we see
Soap for the visible stain
Soap for the unseeable disease

Soap of lovers in a tub
Lathering each other
Soap rubbed on the body for burial
Gather them into your arms
Bring them out to the street

To a basket woven of sweetgrass
Stir until smooth
Stare fear in the eye and call
On the waters and winds to forgive
And cleanse us once and for all.

Switchback

More across than up
we single file
the narrow trail

each turn returning
us the way we came
not so much ahead
or behind
as parallel

an Escher sketch
that goes
both somewhere
and nowhere

when we keep
alert for bear and
deer within the rare
old growth forest

we stumble
on root flare
and outcrop

when we watch
our step
we're lashed

by branches we
feel the animals
watching us pass

a gray cloud
seeps down
the mountain

we can't tell
where one ends
and one begins
or if the cry
is a hawk or a far

siren and now rain
claps the canopy
and ferns on both sides
of the trail
wave us on

to the sunlit
gauntlet of thorny
shrubs covered
in white flowers
their sweetness so
much like a memory
of sweetness
we want to linger
the air drumming
with bees the flowers

crawling with them
the bees don't seem to
care about us but
we know nothing
is straightforward

we move forward
in increments
sideways
by reversal
to the summit
more meadow than peak
the wind parting
the grasses
for the view we came for—
the valley where we live.

II.

Gold

High in a bare tree, the gold mylar balloon—
deflated, string attached—hangs fluttering
from a squirrel's nest. It may have escaped
a child's grasp, floated into the woods
and snagged itself there, but I like to think
the squirrel found it—lying flat on the trail
or twisted in a thicket—succumbed to
its shimmering glint and dragged it, limb by
limb, up the tree to its nest. Chittering
wildly, it unfurled the balloon, sunny flag
of its disposition, then curled up to sleep
beneath the winter sky, where a hawk
floats in widening circles waiting
for something to catch its eye.

When Water Is Up to Here with Us

It will rise over us,
roll in great waves
through our houses
stripping beds,

sheets and pillows
drifting off like jellyfish.

It means to unhang
family pictures, lay
them down beside
the drowned,

carry off the bodies,
the pianos, the aquariums.

Then tetra will swim
with walleye,
eels drape
from ceiling fans

and potted plants nestle
in the limbs of maples.

The large appliances
will float
through doorways
like sea mammals

migrating, following
food, singing to each other.

Mulch

Mothers sometimes find their children
sitting placidly in the garden shoving mulch
into their mouths by the handful.
Down on my knees spreading it like icing
around the yard, breathing the rich, loamy aroma,
I myself am sorely tempted to take a bite.

The word itself is tasty—from old English *melsc*—
mellow, sweet—strawy dung, loose earth, leaves
morphing into middle English *molsh*—soft, moist.
Organic blend of comfort food and love making,
chocolate in bed, soft moans, lift and kneel,
savory smell rising like yeast, steamy as hot bread.

The afterlife of trees—mountains of the felled
and fallen, the cut short and cut down, splintered,
cracked, twisted shadows of themselves, sprigs
of greenery still clinging to the recent arrivals.
Into the maw of colossal machinery, the mountains
sink, transformed in the din to shreds, chips,

nuggets, powder spewed like dark rainbows
into new, rising mountains, heat building inside
the core, smoke without fire ghosting the slopes.
Amid the smoke the shovels move in, scoop
the cooling mulch into the row of trucks waiting
to deliver their dense and porous cargo.

Such variety: pine bark, cypress, cedar, hardwood
blends; natural or dyed (sacrilege)—brown, red, black—
laid out in beds, islands, aprons, halos on the ground,
where halos protect best. Inside a mulch pile I found
five soft, murky eggs. What bird lays eggs in mulch? None,
but more than one kind of snake is drawn to it like Eden.

When the truck pulls up with mulch piled high
on the flatbed, I can't help myself, I run outside
as if the ice cream man has arrived and shout
I love mulch! The driver, wiry, weather worn,
doesn't hear me, or pretends. He rubs his stubble,
nods. *Where you want it dumped?*

Shrine

In the woods I find Buddha
embossed on a green glass disk
leaning against the base of a tree.

Size and heft of a silver dollar,
it feels like my good luck

until the voice in my head that doubts
everything says
Not yours.

I returned it to the tree. Returned every day
to see Buddha still there, plus something new—

first a long crow's feather
tucked behind the disk. Then,

lying in front, five white pebbles
arranged in a crescent.

Then a child's ring appeared,
bejeweled with plastic rubies and emeralds.

On it went, a spontaneous, evolving shrine
enlarged one gesture at a time

like the just-before-sunrise call
and response of birds
you don't see.

Then gone.

Everything. Even the pebbles—

the tree base as empty
as it had been
before the Buddha.

But not empty.

A net of moss, no longer hidden, greener
than the sea glass Buddha, spread out
in all directions

      from the root flare.

Lullaby to a Black Bear

Was it the snow that woke you—
the light of all those tiny swirling
moons that drew you from your den?

The warm fat you packed on all fall
unburned, you pad heavily
through the snow-covered yard,
the thick curtain still coming down,

reshaping everything but you,
every flake vanishing on your fur
as if falling on a dark lake.

Invisible in summer—a shadow,
an absence in plain sight—now
every moment makes you more
apparent, more lustrous.

Black bear inside of snow
inside of night, the world reduced
to black and white is rife with danger.

Turn back, return to your secret
sleep, to the dream I'd have you dream—
a long journey through high mountains
to a bottomless lake.

Famished, scraggly, you stand
at water's edge and drink deeply,
spring's small green waves lapping your feet.

By Campfire

Post apocalypse, if I survive, I'll be no help
rebuilding from the ashes. I can say
electricity, amazing—started with a kite
and lightning, but how it got to houses
I don't know. And the combustion engine—

the places it took us! But with a gun
to my head I couldn't build one. Or the gun,
either, which may be the upside. Phonograph,
telephone, computer, toilet--forget it.
I can't make a square or any other knot

because the night my scout troop earned
that badge, I was faking a stomachache.
I don't know viral from bacterial, but I could
warn of invisible things out to kill us, advise
against leeches as a cure for anything,

suggest that cooked is safer than raw.
With a couple sticks, I could make fire,
I think, and that's no small leap for Man,
but who can't do that? No, if I live beyond
the end, there's little I can do but pass the time

by a campfire with other watery-eyed survivors,
maybe chewing the fat of a rabbit someone knows
how to trap and dress. In gratitude, I might recite
fragments of poems from the old world, smoke
like ghosts rising into the star-dotted night.

Zen Dog

He follows his nose deep into the understory, roots
through thickets and windfall. Returns with the stick
he's chosen—who knows why—from the hundreds of hundreds
in this factory of sticks. He carries it the way a tightrope walker
carries a balance bar. Tail high and plume-like he clenches it,
uphill and down, wherever the trail goes. Clenches it while he lifts
his leg to a tree, while he squats, shits, and back-kicks leaves,
while he stops and listens, head cocked, while he lifts his nose,
nudging the air, nostrils vibrating, while he bursts forth as if from
a starting block to chase a squirrel up a tree. He carries the stick
like a trophy. It is his. Is him. And then, for no apparent reason, mid-
stride he lets it go. It falls as naturally and unpredictably as a branch
from a tree. He goes on, doesn't change pace, doesn't look back.

Horse Not Zebra

When med students are learning
how to diagnose symptoms, they're told
think horse, not zebra — the common, not the exotic.

Which is good advice even if you're not a doctor.
Like when your phone rings at 3:00 in the morning,
think wrong number, not *who died?*

Or if your love is over an hour late
for dinner and hasn't called to explain, think
gridlock, not head-on; dead zone, not dead.

When the guy in the truck doesn't slow down
much less stop when you step into the crosswalk,
think distracted, not son-of-a-bitch. Recall the time

your mind was still at work, how shocked you were
to see in your rearview a woman in the crosswalk
flipping you off with both hands.

And if you're steaming in a mile long backup
because protesters have blocked the bridge again,
don't think where are the damn cops

when you need them, think how,
when popping sounds wake you at night,
you think firecracker, not gun.

Disclosure Statement

It's like talking to police—say as little as possible,
our realtor said when I asked how forthcoming
we should be about the quirks and flaws of our house.
We all laughed, but what I thought was
never in a thousand tries would I have made that analogy.
Not me, encased in my comfortable skin, reassured
to see police driving down our street, waving
when they pass me walking the dog.
The few times I've talked to police I wanted to
tell them more, not less, to be more helpful, say
Yes, I did hear shouting coming from the park,
even if I didn't. Even the time I was arrested
with friends trespassing at Mountain Lake to swim naked
in the freezing water, when the sheriff appeared
and told us to get out and get dressed we were going to jail,
even then I wasn't worried, not really, and when
he asked if there were any more of us, I realized Joyce
was missing and told the sheriff, and we all called for her
until she walked out of the woods angry
at me for giving her up. But I said it was better
to be arrested than be left alone in the woods
with no way back to campus. *I would have found a way*
she hissed in the back of the prowler. In the small town cell,
after the clank of the door—hair still wet, shaking
with cold, after seeing how the redneck deputies
leered at the girls and despised our college kid
air of entitlement—my fear was real, but somehow already

it was fodder for the story that I'd tell at parties
while we passed around a joint. That I'm telling now.
I laughed with our realtor whose art history degree
led him to a job selling houses, who moments before
had asked about the family photos on our walls. I laughed
and said, *I know what you mean*, knowing I didn't
and never could, and that he knew it, too, and I started
to resent his answer, and the silence then that filled the house.

The Bus of History (Montgomery, Alabama, 1963)

Our blue Air Force busses pulled up at one end of the school,
their yellow busses at the other. Every day, sneers in hallways,
staredowns in class. Rosa Parks, the boycott—barely over.

They were rednecks, racists. We were racists, too, but knew better.
Rumor had it that last year, or the year before, after gym we wiped
the smirk off George Wallace, Jr's. face. When the President was shot

during 4th period, they cheered. My friend Cecil slapped his head
and cried, "I just sent him a letter." We single-filed to our buses
hearing their laughter and Rebel yells. The Base was still. Our fathers

didn't come home until long after dinner. Our mothers stared at tv,
clenching tissue. Mine sobbed, "Jackie is holding up better than me."
I took my 7-iron outside to practice my swing, each follow-through

an explosion of dirt and grass. I wasn't angry, or sad, wasn't aware
that the bus of history had caught up with me. I just liked tearing up
the yard, and nobody told me to stop. Before the playoff game

against Jeff Davis, the pep club covered the school with posters:
No Mercy for Rebels! Rebs to the Sword!! Destroy the Rebels.
On game day, a new one appeared—*Peaceful Coexistence*

*With the Rebels--s*oon on the floor, shredded, covered in shoe prints.
On the bus home, Cecil elbowed me, pulled a scrap of the poster
from his book bag and stared at me until I understood that he

had made it. He started laughing his loud, annoying laugh, laughed
so hard he started coughing, then gasping, until he found
his inhaler, jammed it in his mouth, sucked hard, and held his breath.

Expecting Lowell

We're two weeks premature, you're one week late,
and the pandemic that began when you were conceived
is still growing. Grandparents-in-waiting, we do
the only thing we can—walk daily to the sprawling cemetery

shaded by live oaks as twisty and old as Savannah itself,
a forest of monuments with designated picnic spots,
families and dogs welcome, waste bags provided.
We walk across centuries, from the earliest war to the latest,

from yellow fever to scarlet, Spanish flu to Covid-19.
We linger at the children's graves, the little marble lambs.
We add stones to the Jewish stones, wander the Irish section
to the intersecting paths of founding families and nouveau riche.

All the city's dead were welcome as long as they weren't Black.
We take our time, plague time, the toll approaching the Civil
War's—one side amply represented here, the air so dense
with ghosts we call it humidity to keep from seeing them.

Against all reason and the monuments to history ignoring itself,
repeating like the ocean groaning at the cemetery's edge,
we place our trust in babies—our mulligans, do-overs for our muffed
selves—hoping to get it right this time. At last, on New Year's Day

you arrive—the only one without a mask—caramel-colored
more perfect union of black and white, your parents
repeating the clear and dark liquids of your name. Little Lowell,
how in this world can I not overflow unequally with joy and fear

and wishful thinking? I imagine you running between the cemetery's
ancient trees and the rolling graves, chased only by your own dog
to the overgrown path that leads to an unobstructed view of the ocean.
I see you breathing easy in the crowded air. I see you breathing.

Washing Dishes at the Arsenal

The first building, a mile inside the gate,
churned out bullets for side arms and rifles.
Farther in, behind thick bunkers, the bomb factory
squatted, unmarked. Not so much as a Danger sign.
Everything was danger, even the cafeteria, smallest
and most remote building, where I washed dishes
one summer, long-haired college kid with a peace sign
and marijuana leaf patched to my jeans. It was crazy
working there, but the government paid well
and my dad, retired colonel, pulled some strings. I pulled
dirty dishes off the conveyor, loaded and shoved
the wash racks into a metal box as long as my body,
waited for it to lurch out the other side through a blast
of hot air, then unpacked and stacked the steaming dishes.
A tower of plates slipped from my grasp once, the explosion
so loud that everyone in the dining room dove for cover.
When I opened the kitchen door, nobody spoke, but I saw
what they wanted to say. Anti-war protesters showed up
outside the gate sometimes, shaking their signs at traffic.
They looked like me. I kept my eyes on the billboard
that showed how many days since the last accident,
the tall metal numbers like the ones on scoreboards.
I had nothing to do with the accidents they meant, but I took
a certain pride. I made a sign for the kitchen —*Days Without
Breaking A Dish*. Then Building 5 blew. One dead. Would have
been more, but they knew how to limit a blast, localize damage.
All they found was the guy's Texas-shaped belt buckle.

I kept seeing it—rocketing in the air, lying inside a casket.
When the arsenal reopened, the billboard still said *703 Days*
Without An Accident. But the next morning it was *1 Days*....
Even more than the buckle, the sign threw me so off balance
that I pulled over and sat there staring at it. How many days
had I held the dead man's dishes in my hands—
scraped, rinsed, loaded, and stacked them?

By the time summer ended, the protests were big and frequent.
Cars turning into the arsenal were stoned. I didn't want to think
about it. I wanted my own car when I went back to school.
I'd earned it. My last day at the arsenal was the forty-seventh
without an accident, even longer without a broken dish.

Perfect Work

When I consider how my working life's
been spent, I think fondly of driving
the Floyd County bookmobile—an old school
bus refitted with rows of shelves and a built-in
desk behind the driver's seat so I could swivel

smoothly from driver to librarian.
I see myself gripping the wheel, chugging
narrow mountain roads,
navigating hairpins to the parking lot
of Andy's Summit Mart where they wait—
three or four kids running around, grandmas
smoking and shouting at the kids
to settle, and the wiry man in the tractor cap
off to one side like he may or may not be here
to browse the war books.

I always hesitate
before opening the door, a pause
to let everyone, including me, absorb
the marvel before us—a moveable feast,
other worlds on wheels, three steps above
the top of the towering mountain.

Now, when I slouch into my office, down
on the world or myself, especially the days
I don't think I can stand one more stab at my work,
I imagine the bookmobile crossing the New River
through clouds, past meadows and pastures, cows
as my witness, my heavy cargo leaning back,
me leaning forward, looking for the parking lot
shining in the sun like a small lake.
How I wish I had gotten that job—never thankless
or boring, never less than fulfilling.

Aubade with Bear

As reluctant as I to leave, night leaves
behind a remnant, a black bear

hugging the shoulder of our street, plodding
toward the woods beyond the creek—

each cooling streetlight it passes
flashing briefly bright again.

IV.

All Evidence

It's hard to tell which we'll kill first,
ourselves or nature. If nature hangs on
until we're glowing dust, it can start

over, all evidence of us disappearing
like the tattered birthday balloon a squirrel
hoisted to its nest and unfurled like a flag.

Or the bits of wire, dryer lint, and human
hair the wren weaves into her nest
tucked between our eave and downspout.

But where will the field mice winter
when our walls tumble down? What will
swifts do without chimneys? Black bears

without leftover KFC and pizza
driving them unwild? Nature will miss us
when we're gone—no one to hear a tree

fall or step into a river, no gleaming
baubles crows crave. No one to praise
the snow. Nothing for wind to chime.

Based on Actual Events

Not long into the movie my wife says,
We've seen this before, and I say, *No*,
but I can tell by the way she leans toward
the television that she doesn't believe me.
Maybe you saw it one night when I was out,
I say as the head of the former Nazi
doctor disappears between the Mossad agent's
spread legs, his examination just starting
when she slams her legs shut and stabs
a syringe into his neck, then clamps tighter
while he tries to wrest his head from her
crotch, until the drug kicks in and his limp
body slips to the floor.

I would have remembered this, I say, a little
more smugly than I intend. She shrugs
and calls the dog over for a grooming session.
It's night in a derelict East Berlin flat
where the Nazi is tied to a radiator and hard rain
falls outside. Falls inside, too, from multiple
ceiling cracks. Not that it matters since the Nazi
will be smuggled out of the country within hours.
Even so, the hardened, trained-to-kill agent
rummages in the kitchen just like an ordinary person
and emerges with pots, carefully placing one
beneath each leak. The plinks create a syncopated tune

that's almost sweet, but we know the Nazi has cut
his ropes with a shard of crockery and is just waiting.

As the agent moves around placing the pots, I get
a wave of déjà vu, and during the drip ditty
I know for sure I have seen this movie before,
though I remember nothing but this moment
of domestic problem-solving and the plinking rain.
I turn to Stephanie, but she is absorbed in the dog,
checking his ears for mites. The Nazi sees his chance
and slashes a long, deep wound across the agent's face,
kicks her viciously, repeatedly, and vanishes out the door.
And I think yes, we've seen this show, many times—
good and evil in their eternal war, so familiar

I don't remember it, not the titillating sexual headlock,
not the gruesome violence, not the ending in which—
spoiler alert—good prevails this time.
I only remember the nerves-of-ice agent suddenly
becoming as real and flawed as anyone, doing what anyone
would do—catch the dripping rain, and enjoy a little
unexpected music. I know I should tell Stephanie
she was right, but I don't want to admit I was wrong
any more than the Mossad agent will admit that she
let the Nazi escape. Instead, she concocts a lie that never stops
torturing her. I slip my arm around Stephanie, and when
she asks *do you remember any of this yet?* I smile and pull her
closer to me, knowing she knows.

Biography of My Name

People guess I'm from a line of Vikings or Saxons.
Eric the Red. Admiral Nelson. Glory and gore in my blood,
a Jute's nose. But Nelson is an Ellis Island amputation

of something long and guttural that started with *Nel*
and ended in *stein.* Latvian. Four refugee brothers huddled
in steerage. A line of shopkeepers. Abraham landed

in a Pennsylvania coal town where he opened a dry goods
store, married the seamstress Anna Rosenberg and fathered
six children. The youngest, Daveed, my father, delivered

groceries on a horse he named Tommy. Eric came from
my mother—mixed English, Irish, Welsh—pure Quaker
by the time she was born near Washington's Crossing.

Even more than most of her Rosie-the-Riveter cohort,
she was devoted to the red, white and blue, her substitute
for religion. She didn't trust anything she couldn't see,

and what she saw was the backside of faith
when she and my father announced their intention—
her New and his Old Testament families turning on them.

That's why she liked Eric, swaddled me in its pagan creed.
No Peter or Paul for her. No Saul or Jacob, either.
For me, a name for the middle of America.

Blue Birds

Way out in the country there's a meadow
filled with old Blue Bird school busses, hundreds
of them, parked side by side, rust crusting
the bumpers, vines crawling over them tugging
downward. But let's not dwell,

every bus has its last stop.
Graveyards abound. We go knowingly,
seated if we're lucky, hoping to cruise, braced
for ruts, playing tic-tac-toe in our breath
on the window, aware it's always a cat's game.

I say drive me to my final rest in one of those
Blue Birds, everyone singing *do-wah-diddy* like we did
in band a million Fridays ago coming and going
to games. Win or lose, we sang. Sang
ourselves beyond ourselves, one state to another.

Graying

The novelty intrigued at first –
a gray hair! Yanked it out. Examined.
Coarser than the brown. Crimpy. Like a pubic hair
that lost its spring, and way.

As they filled my temples, I thought, *distinguished*.
I thought, *salt and pepper*. Little by little,
my temples were all salt,
my sideburns pillars of it. I thought, *old*.

A good friend — who else — said
You've gone gray so fast!
I leaned forward like an old silverback gorilla,
pressed my weight onto my knuckles. Grunted.

In front of the mirror, clear as a stream
above the mist, I think, *how vain,*
I'm thinking of dyeing my hair. It's summer,
if it's disaster, I won't have to endure my students'
and colleagues' undisguised contempt. I'll stay inside
until it grows out.

I decide to wait until I return
from seeing my dad in Florida.
When I pull into the parking lot
at the assisted living place where he is dying,
a few old men are walking the perimeter,

gray heads down, watching their steps,
one of them smiling.
I run my hand through my hair, check
myself in the rearview. I think,
This is what happens. If you're lucky.

Play Ball or Sing

When I heard that the person who prepares
your order at Subway is called a sandwich artist,

I remembered my childhood ambition to be a singer.
Standing in the outfield with my glove like a dead flower

drooping from my wrist, I sang originals, composed
on the fly—extended odes to thunder and loneliness.

When the batter connected and the ball lofted
toward me, I had no idea where it would land.

I watched and waited, my song caught in my throat
until the ball hit the grass and rolled far behind me

while the crowd screamed, but not how I'd imagined.
Is it possible to be an artist and make a sandwich

at the same time, or is it inescapable that you play ball
or you sing, but you can't do both?

Rilke, Vincent, Emily—to name a few—couldn't
hold a job if they wanted to, and lucky for us, they didn't.

It's the old question of money, or worth. The question
of paying the bills and dining out once in a while, or

singing for your supper like the buskers downtown,
their starveling dogs curled on the sidewalk beside them.

The answers aren't as important as the questions,
someone is always saying. I say, *What the hell?*

I could use answers now that my brain is starting
to ossify and a question mark looks like a rope

just long enough to hang myself with. Right now,
for example, I can tell by her face and body

language that my sandwich artist hates my bougie
guts for asking if I can get some mayo

on the side, could she go easy on the olives,
and does this come with chips, or is that extra?

About Black Bears

First thing to know is that they're shy.
Wanting nothing to do with us
has served them well, flourishing far
beyond the aggressive grizzly and polar.
Easily scared off with shouts and pots,
they're less prone to attack than a dog.
If you wander too near, they hope
to frighten you with a huff and a bluff
charge and loud smacking of lips.

That surge of fear you feel—don't
dismiss it, no matter how often
bears have fled from you. They will
kill you, easily, if they choose.
As they do on rare occasions.
You won't know it's not a bluff
until it's not. You won't outrun it—
they lope at 30 miles-per-hour.
You won't be saved by water—
they like water and swim like whales.

If you suspect a bear is near,
look up as well as around.
It may be perched on a limb
like the king of crows,
silent but for the whispery
hiss of claws scoring bark.

You can't run, neither can you hide.
Their sense of smell is seven times
sharper than a bloodhound's.

Do not play dead. That might work
with a brown, but your best chance
with a black bear is to fight.
They're smart, they don't like to fight.
Among their mysterious ways,
they don't claim territory, they share
their range with their kind.
The size of a small car, they move
as silently as cats. They turn
invisible at will, shadows of themselves
on a sunlit street. They open doors —
car, house, garage, refrigerator —
without thumbs. They thrive among us,
wandering our streets like the holy poor
in search of sustenance and peace.
Science can't explain how
they developed the good sense
to den through winter, shutting down

all bodily functions but birth. No wonder
they are gods in many cultures.
Bestowers of courage and strength.
Creators of the universe. From which,
in their wisdom, they withdrew
and turned into the stars we connect.
When they die, they live on

at the center of galaxies, black holes
we call them, pulling us
relentlessly toward them.

V.

Mysteries of the Ellipsis

In punctuation's trinity
what is there
is what is not there . . . tips

of tongues and icebergs,
remnants of a breadcrumb trail,
the celestial hunter's belt . . .

three peepholes in a textured wall,
the little that allows for more,
the telegraph's untapped news . . .

connected, the dots reveal
both the hidden and the big
picture . . . the better left unsaid.

Dark Evergreen

In her invitation to the gathering
in honor of our dead friend, the host
says grief shared is grief lessened.
I believe it, but all I want to do is walk
in the woods alone, the way an animal
goes off to lick its wounds. Kneel to anguish,
Rilke said, don't squander grief—our dark
evergreen—trying to see the end.

Rilke was a jerk, said Berryman. Probably,
but that doesn't mean he was wrong.
Evergreens keep the woods dark and cool,
constant as a cave. I follow the trail. Leave
the trail. Lose myself but not my loss. Before
the wound can heal, it must be made deeper.

Parade

When the ice cream truck drives up the street
toodling its happy song, the neighbors
come out, get their flavor and quickly disappear.
But when a black bear saunters up the street,
the neighbors come out and the parade begins,
the bear leading, drifting from one shoulder to the other,
checking trashcans for smells that need investigation.
The growing crowd follows, phones in hand,
taking stills and videos, whispering excitedly, swapping
bear stories, laughing, parents telling kids to stay
out of the way of the guy riding a bike in figure eights,
the line stopping short when the bear glances over its shoulder,
regards its followers with a blend of curiosity and disdain,
then keeps leading the parade, ignoring the dogs losing
their minds behind fences, ignoring cars driving toward it.
The cars stop, the occupants watch the spectacle pass
and sometimes leave their cars and join the crowd. Eventually
the bear glides off the street, down a slope, behind a house
to who knows where. It simply vanishes. Parade's end.
The new family on the block rushes from their backyard
exclaiming it walked right past them, not three feet away
as they sat on their deck having wine and hummus.
They thought the bear was going to take the bowl!
The parade disbands slowly, everyone meandering
back to their house, their dinner, their ice cream.
Sharing their photos and videos as they go.

Never Good

Whenever someone around my age drops dead
by heart attack or stroke, I say, *That's how I want to go*—
as if it's a bold idea, possibly controversial, like everyone else
would prefer a slow descent into diapers and drooling,
strapped upright in a wheelchair, life draining away
like water in a clogged sink.

Is there anyone who doesn't want a quick death
while they're still in good health? Who wouldn't give up
some years of life to spare themselves and loved ones
a long series of indignities on the way to a pitiful end?

My brother-in-law died in bed, asleep, healthy, 70 years old,
no signs in the days or hours before that anything was wrong.
Asleep beside him, his wife heard and felt nothing the moment
he went from alive to dead—not a gasp or shudder, not her own
body warning her with a chilling dream. She slept right through

the usual routine—not waking to the smell of coffee he made
first thing in the morning, not hearing kibbles fall into the dog's bowl,
the dog's tags clinking against the metal bowl. Her eyes didn't open
until sunlight rose high enough to slip between the blinds.

She sensed the lump of him under the covers, but she didn't
think *dead*, she thought *overslept*, and nudged him.
The feel of him was wrong. The current of fear flicked on,

surged, and she burst out of bed to his side, his head
on the pillow looking deeply asleep, but not quite. Something off
about the skin, the tone and stillness. She held her palm to his cheek.

He didn't suffer, I tell her. *It was a good death.*
Not for me, she says. *We weren't finished. Give him back.*
I'll pay—I don't care. Anything. Anything for goodbye.

Scouts

Those who are gone from us—
I hate calling them
the dead. It makes them seem
so serious, if not symbolic, so heavy
with the knowledge they carry.
Let's not forget that those who left
were lighthearted and surprising:
my mother at the dinner table
pulling a derringer from a hidden pocket
and shooting her grandson in the forehead
with a single, sharp bullet of water. This
after a day of the boy sneaking up
on aunts and cousins and drenching them
in rapid fire super-soaker. He was pleased
with his mischief but not as pleased as
the family when Granny meted out justice.
The boy, she said, had been *a horse's rosette*,
her vivid euphemism for asshole.

This morning I woke early in the dark
with a terrible ache to talk to her again,
thirty years since she went to her Great Reward,
a term she favored for its irony
since she believed that the Reward is a choice
between going up in smoke
or lying deep in the dirt, both of which
sounded better to her than pearly gates

and eternal perfect boredom.
I don't know why I wanted so badly
to hear her strong voice, her robust laughter.
Or why it was suddenly important to ask her
about the origin of *horse's rosette* since I've never
heard anyone but her and all of her descendants,
including me, brandish it like a coat of arms.
Of course, she didn't tell me, but I heard
her voice, heard her say, *Scouts, call us scouts.*
And it made sense, the ones who go ahead

to make sure the trail is clear, the water safe.
The ones who leave signals for the rest—
a white ribbon tied to a cactus, an arrow
painted on a boulder with beet juice, a secret
word carved into a tree. When I ask her
if she left signs for me, her laughter ricochets
in my head like a bullet echoing across a canyon.

Rules of the Body, A Partial List

Don't be a dick, a pussy, an asshole, a pain
in the butt. Don't stick your neck out
or bite off more than you can chew.

Keep your nose clean and to the grindstone,
your head on straight, or down,
or up, depending. But not up your ass.

Keep your ear to the ground, eye on the ball,
finger on the pulse. Take heart and have a heart.
Give a piece of your mind.

Bite your tongue. Button your lip.
Face the truth and the music. Lend an ear
and a hand. Turn the other cheek.

Stay on your toes. Put your foot down,
your best foot forward, not in your mouth.
Get a leg up. Break a leg. Have balls

or grow a pair. Take a deep breath. Give a shit.
Cross your fingers and your heart.
Hope to die.

Disappearing

The dentist says there's no reason
to replace the tooth I lost.
My skin tone fades and fades to match my hair.
I grow down the doorframe--shorter
and shorter until I'm not seen. Passersby greet my dog
as if it were alone. Next in line, I watch
the bank teller ask who's next.
Someone bumps me and says, *Sorry, I didn't see you.*
Another shudders past like he's hit a patch of cold air.

On the plus side, eavesdropping's easy.
And nobody asks me to help lift anything.
I'm never singled out as a person of interest.
Animals pay me no mind. I nearly touched a deer
before it noticed. A Great Horned Owl
didn't budge as I stepped closer.
Face to face, I saw that it was scanning
the meadow behind me.
Black bears brush by me like sleepwalkers
on their way to the feeders in my backyard.
The spooked birds fly right through me.

Avoiding the Dog

You don't hear it over your bike's winding
engine, don't see it until it's almost on you,
spit-glistened jaws snapping.

Your first impulse is speed, outrunning,
but it's already adjusted, angled
to intercept you at the turn you can't avoid.

You imagine kicking it into a yelping heap
when it leaps for your calf, but that takes balance
and timing you don't have.

Your only hope is to make yourself
slow down, resist the urge to veer away, and watch
for its shoulders to roll, neck stretch

for the lunge—then lower your head, tighten
your wrist and snap the throttle.
If you don't pinwheel across the blacktop,

glance back at the dog falling away like a movie
running backwards, toward the old, familiar house
with sagging porch, where it started.

My Brothers

I was walking home from school.
Across the street two older boys —
high schoolers my sisters knew
and didn't like — stood slugging it out
on the sidewalk, really going after
each other — torn shirts, blood, headlocks,
kidney punches. I watched, absorbed
and afraid that somehow I'd be pulled
into their whirlwind of flailing and cursing,
their boyness, hard as the brothers I didn't have.
A car drove past, slowed, kept going.
Another slowed, pulled over. A man
in a tan uniform got out and yelled.
The boys bolted for the hedges.
The man looked at me and asked if I was okay.
I didn't know what he meant. I nodded.
He got into his car and drove off.
I looked to the empty place where the boys
and car and man had been. It felt like
trying to call back a dream.
And here they came, staggering from the hedge,
laughing. They took their places on the sidewalk.
One of them smeared something near his mouth
as red as the lipstick my sister once spread across
my pursed lips. The other boy shouted
at me, *Did it look real?* A car was coming.
They grabbed each other and started fighting.
I saw how it was done. The car slowed down.
I was ready, if it stopped, to run.

VI.

Beating Myself Up

In the bathroom mirror I see my eye
swollen, discolored, a blood encrusted cut
woven into the brow.
I touch it, wince, remember last night in bed,
the fresh sheet tucked so tightly at my feet
it took both hands to loosen it—
until my grip slipped and I landed myself
a knockout punch.

After all the times I've beaten myself up
for my failures of character—
mean-spirited remarks, lies,
acts of kindness withheld—
the never-ending list,

this time I did it literally, and better
yet, for no good reason.
My own archaic, lumpy torso
reflected harshly in the vanity light,
already I'm changing
the story—maybe an elbow in a pickup game.
Maybe a bar fight with loudmouths
who wouldn't walk away.

I'm hoping that friends say I might need stitches.
I'll shrug, modest as ever. *It's nothing*, I say
to my image. Knowing when the bruise and cut
are gone, I'll only have myself to blame.

Their Romance

His nature was to look down,
hers to look up.
They both loved mountains.

He was drawn
to her sense of humor.
She liked his laugh.

Gardening, she was
herbs and veggies.
He was flowers and grasses.

She drove with both feet, right
for gas, left for brake. He shifted
so smoothly she felt nothing.

Her mistake—believing him
when he swore
he was a bad liar.

After the fight
she outslept the cat.
He read all his spam.

His safe word
was *and*.
Hers, *but*.

At the opening, he watched
the door. She watched
the guy with the drink tray.

Looking into her eyes
he saw the sky. That blue.
That far away.

When he stopped trying too hard
to make her want him again,
she still didn't want him.

Twelfth Night

Above the tree line, the Waffle House sign
shines brilliantly, no less a beacon than the star
three kings chased to arrive on the twelfth night
after the miraculous birth, the night of the birthday

of Stephanie. A dozen eggs glow like twelve moons
over the grill where the cook clinks his spatula tune
shoving hash browns into mounds.

On the night of the birthday of Stephanie,
watching her study the luminous menu,
my epiphany occurs: the sky is not the limit—

time means nothing—breakfast, lunch, and dinner
spread out before us.
We can have it all, any time, and we do.

Not the full-of-itself moon in the window, nor
the crazed frost glittered on the sidewalk,
nor the lamb-white light humming in the ceiling
are more radiant and necessary than she.

The Day She Left

The instant he steps from the car's
cool interior into the August heat,
his glasses fog over. He walks
to the house trusting memory and baby steps.
Hands scanning the air like antennae,
he avoids the ugly metal pig she insisted
was adorable, misses the concrete bench
that came with the house, steps over
the bulging root of the maple tree
and the broken paver he meant to replace.
He gropes his way up the three porch steps
to the door, feels the key into the lock,
and enters the house, smiling and turning
his head as if waiting for someone to come
and hear what he had done.
The gray clouds still floating before his eyes.

Live Like a Bear Is Near

I sometimes tell people I pass on the street
that I just saw a bear a couple blocks back. It's a lie,
but true to the bears I have seen, like the one
that hoisted itself over a privacy fence and landed
on its front legs, back legs waggling the air like
someone learning to dive. Steadied, it drifted
to the middle of the street, tracked the white line
to the playground where no children played, slipped
behind a hedge and disappeared. No one saw it but me
and a black cat that fled, hackles up, Halloween style.

I love the sudden thrill that flashes on their faces.
They pull their earbuds out and scan the area, deciding
if they'll go the way of the cat, or stay the course. Most
keep going, fully alert, maybe for the first time
noticing both the brilliant green moss filling the sidewalk gaps,
and the highest limb of the sycamore stretching
like a tightrope to the cracked attic window across the street.

They listen like they haven't listened since they were teens
sneaking out of the house. They listen for the thunk of a trash bin,
for tumbled cans and bottles, for a shout or a howl. They squint
at every dark shape and shadow, become themselves as silent
as bears, attuned to smallest vibrations. When they don't see

the bear that was never there, they are equal parts relieved
and disappointed, aroused by the force of mixed feelings.
They stand on the corner waiting for someone to come along,
eager to warn them to beware, a bear is near.

The Runners

I'm not a runner but I love to watch them—
their mute glide, raindrop footfalls, arms
rhythmic as wings. And I love how they bring
the city to a stop with their K's—the 3's, 5's, and 10's,
the Fun Run, the Jingle Bell, the Firecracker—
everybody wearing red white and blue—
streets blocked, blue police lights not sparking fear,
volunteers at tables checking names,
handing out numbers, synchronizing watches.

Young moms in full stride push strollers cargoed
with wide-eyed babies. Dads run beside kids
giving advice, watching for fatigue, ready to swoop
them up and keep running. Old folks, papery but fit,
move wisely, unperturbed as turtles. The serious
athletes, straight-faced, burst quickly to the front,
their gaze more inward than out, personal best
on their minds. Behind them, the big bunch paces itself,
amorphous as a bulge squeezing through a snake's length.

Then, for a while, it seems over, the end
come and gone before you know it until finally the finalists
appear, some talking and laughing, some alone, limping,
likely to be picked off by cheetahs—those beautiful runners—
if this were the Serengeti. But this is America, so we cheer
for their never-say-die gumption, knowing that some day
the last shall be first. But not today.

The crowd drifts away. Tables get folded and loaded
onto trucks. The police cut their blue lights, give
their sirens a half-whoop, and return to circling the city
returning to itself—loud, clumsy, in a hurry.

Bus Real

The best time of our time in Madrid, love,
was not the Prado, the Palace, the Plaza Mayor,
not the Reina Sophia, the Rastro, Retiro Park—
but the night we decided to ride the bus
through every corner of the city, the lively and bright
as well as the shadowy and still, the people
boarding and leaving in a gush and clamor—
families fumbling down the aisle, young couples
with their mouths all over each other, old women in black
with fans, old men in black with bags, all the dark-haired,
dark-eyed Madrileños who siesta by day
and take the bus at night to street cafes for olives and tapas,
Real Madrid's stadium brilliant in the distance.
Remember how we moved forward whenever
seats opened up until we were eye level with the back
of the driver's head, staring at the corkscrews of hair
on his collar as if they were another attraction?
When the bus stopped at a corner where no one was waiting
we listened to the shuffling behind us, faint footsteps down
and out the rear exit while we waited for whatever
was next, the whole city thumping in the pulse of our held hands.
The driver turned to us and we saw his face for the first time,
how tired he was, how much older than we thought.
He pushed the lever that opened the door, made a sweeping
after you gesture, and we realized we were the only ones
on the bus, that we'd reached the literal end of the line.
He turned off the headlights, ceiling lights, engine, the bus

groaning into its final stop. We smiled and wished him both
buenas noches and *buenos dias* as he waved us away toward sunrise.
The spotlit monuments led us to our hotel where we devoured
warm rolls and café con leche before we fell into our bed
and slept deep into the day, all the way through our tour
of the Basilica, which we'd heard is stunning, not to be missed.

Blind Mover

He walked the house once,
another mover beside him naming
the rooms, then returned to the truck
and emerged with a tower of boxes
stacked higher than his head, his ear
pressed against cardboard as if listening
to something inside guide him
down the ramp, across the yard and through
the front door. Again and again.
He wasn't the biggest of them, but the others
called him for help with the heaviest lifts—
the sleeper couch, the chests of drawers,
the concrete garden bench. Something
about his certainty against all logic.
If I moved with his grace and assurance
through the world I see, never mind
the invisible distractions of my own making,
I wouldn't have feared him—feared for him
I meant to say—wouldn't have touched
his arm, wouldn't have tried to save him
from a threshold he knew better than I.
My gesture made him flinch, the tower lean
away from him before he righted it
and walked through the door, saying nothing
when I apologized for surprising him.
I should not have been surprised
when the crew boss told me they all

bowl together once a month, and everyone
wants Vincent on their team—strike
after strike rolling from his fingertips.

The Creature

Barely a month old and already
everyone wants a piece of him.
Uncle Ed says those eyes are mine.
Aunt Nancy can't stop holding his hands
because they're her mother's *exactly*.

Beth sees his chin every time she looks in the mirror.
The grandparents on one side say it's the family nose.
The other grands pull back their hair
to show how their ears match his.
That mouth belongs to Robin, distant cousin on nobody's side.
Mom and Dad glance at each other.
A well-meaning friend chimes in—he's a perfect blend,
I don't see either of you in him.

Get used to it, kid, everybody wants something from you.
And they'll swear they're giving you a gift.
You were born knowing how to cry, just like the rest of us.
Learning to laugh is work. When you do, it's all yours.
May it be robust and generous.

Acknowledgments

My thanks to the editors of the journals where the following poems first appeared:

2River: "Clearing the Air," "When Water Is Up to Here with Us"

Autumn Sky Poetry Daily: "The Runners"

B O D Y: "The Creature"

Juniper: "Blue Birds"

MacQueen's Quinterly: "Disappearing," "Play Ball or Sing"

Mid-American Review: "Mysteries of the Ellipsis"

New Madrid: "Avoiding the Dog," "The Day She Left"

One: "Almost Enough"

One Art: "My Brothers," "Sheltered in Place"

Prime Number: "Scouts"

Southern Poetry Review: "Blind Mover"

The Sun: "Graying"

Tar River Poetry: "Disclosure Statement"

Valparaiso Poetry Review: "Live Like a Bear Is Near"

Verse-Virtual: "Baton," "Horse Not Zebra," "Soap Spell"

It would take pages to name all the writers, editors, friends, family, students, and colleagues I wish to thank for their support, advice, and love. I'm limiting myself to these few and apologize to those I've had to leave out for lack of space. A great debt of gratitude to these beautiful writers/friends who have helped shape these poems and thus this entire book: David Graham, Andrew Clark, Pam Baggett, Rebecca Baggett, Maggie Anderson, Katherine Soniat, Jessica Jacobs, Nickole Brown, Luke Hankins, Gary Hawkins, Rachel Shopper, Art Stringer, Phil Deal, Tommy Hays, and Diane Lockward from Terrapin Books.

And to steadfast friends for decades: Mark Hudson, Richard Flynn, Rebecca Kennerly, Laura Milner, Dixie Aubrey, Mark Dallas, Phyllis Dallas, Mary Marwitz, Deb Miller, Bob Miller, Ellen Boyle, Steve Jones, Grace Bauer, and Jeanne Larsen.

And to more recent but no less important friends: Alida Woods, Bill Caldwell, Paige Gilchrist, Lou Giron, Dana Lichty, Kathy Nelson, Ginger Graziano, Karen Luke Jackson, Billie Lofland, Judy McAfee, Lucy Thompson, Woody Thompson, Lucy Bowen, Larry Bowen, Connie Hays, and Emily Gill.

Extra love, pride, and gratitude to my son Benny and my daughter Claire, and to their partners Rachel Bradford and Chris Cartright.

Endless thanks to my sisters Alix Jones and Ruth Cuzzort, who did their best to teach their little brother how to dance and to be a decent person; and in memory of my parents—David and Emma Nelson—true models of strength of character and generosity of spirit.

And last but first, profound gratefulness and love to my wife, Stephanie Tames, whose style, creativity, humor, and love have sustained me for forty-two years and counting.

About the Author

Eric Nelson taught writing and literature courses for twenty-six years at Georgia Southern University, where he received the Ruffin Cup in 2009 for sustained excellence in teaching, publishing, and service. He retired, professor emeritus, in 2015, and moved to Asheville, North Carolina, where he teaches part time in the Great Smokies Writing Program at the University of North Carolina Asheville. His six previous poetry collections include *Terrestrials*, chosen by Maxine Kumin for the X. J. Kennedy Award; *The Interpretation of Waking Life*, winner of the University of Arkansas Poetry Award; and *Some Wonder*, which won the 2015 Gival Press Poetry Award.

www.ericnelsonpoet.com